Lost and Found

by Peter Jacobson
illustrated by John Hovell

Practice Decodable 76

McGraw Hill Education

Bothell, WA • Chicago, IL • Columbus, OH • New York, NY

MHEonline.com

Send all inquiries to:
McGraw-Hill Education
8787 Orion Place
Columbus, OH 43240

ISBN: 978-0-02-144779-4
MHID: 0-02-144779-9

Printed in China.

8 9 10 11 12 DSS 27 26 25 24 23

"I lost Grouch!" Rachel shouted. She started to run around the house.

"Grouch, Grouch," she called loudly.

In the den, Rachel looked under a couch.

"No Grouch there," she said. Then Rachel bounced up.

Rachel checked around her room.

"Ouch!" Rachel bumped her head. She still did not find Grouch!

"How about in the kitchen?" Rachel asked. Rachel crouched down. She looked under the fridge.

Rachel looked on the kitchen counter. There was a squeaking sound. The sound was behind a can of flour.

"I found Grouch!" shouted Rachel.

She had Grouch in her hands. Grouch was Rachel's pet mouse.

Practice Decodable 76

Lost and Found

High-Frequency Words Reviewed in Practice Decodable 76

about
around

Previously Reviewed High-Frequency Words

a	could	her	no	that	were
after	day	here	now	the	what
all	did	him	of	their	when
am	do	his	old	them	where
an	don't	how	on	then	will
and	down	I	one	there	with
any	every	if	or	they	would
are	for	in	out	this	yes
as	from	is	over	to	you
ask	get	it	pretty	too	
at	girl	its	red	two	
away	go	jump	ride	up	
be	going	just	right	very	
big	good	know	said	walk	
blue	got	like	saw	want	
brown	green	little	see	was	
but	had	long	she	water	
call	has	look	six	way	
came	have	make	sleep	we	
can	he	me	some	well	
come	help	my	take	went	

Sound/Spelling Correspondences in Practice Decodables

1. Pre-decodable
2. Pre-decodable
3. Pre-decodable
4. Pre-decodable
5. Pre-decodable
6. /s/ spelled *s*,
/m/ spelled *m*,
/a/ spelled *a*
7. /t/ spelled *t, tt*
8. Review
9. /d/ spelled *d*
10. /n/ spelled *n*
11. /i/ spelled *i*
12. /h/ spelled *h_*
13. /p/ spelled *p*
14. /l/ spelled *l, ll*
15. /o/ spelled *o*
16. /b/ spelled *b*
17. /k/ spelled *c*
18. special spelling *al, all*
19. /k/ spelled *k,* ■*ck*
20. /r/ spelled *r*
21. /f/ spelled *f, ff*
22. /s/ spelled *ss*
23. /g/ spelled *g*
24. /j/ spelled *j*
25. /j/ spelled ■*dge*
26. /u/ spelled *u*
27. /z/ spelled *z, zz*
28. /z/ spelled *_s*
29. /ks/ spelled ■*x*
30. /e/ spelled *e*
31. *-ed* ending: /ed/, /d/
32. *-ed* ending: /t/
33. /e/ spelled *_ea_*
34. /sh/ spelled *sh*
35. /th/ spelled *th*
36. /ch/ spelled *ch,* ■*tch*
37. /or/ spelled *or, ore*
38. /ar/ spelled *ar*
39. /w/ spelled *w_*
40. /w/ spelled *wh_*
41. /er/ spelled *er, ir*
42. /er/ spelled *ur*
43. /er/ spelled *ear*
44. /ng/ spelled ■*ng*
45. Schwa
46. *-le, -el, -il, -al*
47. /nk/ spelled ■*nk*
48. /kw/ spelled *qu_*
49. /y/ spelled *y_*
50. /v/ spelled *v*
51. /ā/ spelled *a, a_e*
52. /ī/ spelled *i, i_e*
53. /s/ spelled *ce, ci_*
54. /j/ spelled *ge, gi_*
55. /ō/ spelled *o, o_e*
56. /ū/ spelled *u, u_e*
57. /ē/ spelled *e, e_e*
58. /ē/ spelled *ee, ea*
59. /ē/ spelled *_y, _ie_*
60. /ē/ spelled *_ey*
61. /s/ spelled *cy*
62. /ā/ spelled *ai_, _ay*
63. /ī/ spelled *_igh*
64. /ī/ spelled *_y, _ie*
65. /ō/ spelled *oa_, _ow*
66. /ū/ spelled *_ew, _ue*
67. /m/ spelled *_mb*
68. /n/ spelled *kn_, gn*
69. /r/ spelled *wr_*
70. /f/ spelled *ph*
71. /o͞o/ spelled *oo*
72. /o͞o/ spelled *u, _ue*
73. /o͞o/ spelled *_ew, u_e*
74. /oo/ spelled *oo*
75. /ow/ spelled *ow*
76. /ow/ spelled *ou_*

SRA Open Court Reading

Practice Decodables

Grade 1
Practice Decodable 76
Lost and Found

MHEonline.com

978-0-02-144779-4
MHID 0-02-144779-9

McGraw Hill Education

Hills of Fuzz

by Tamera Williams
illustrated by Kersti Frigell

McGraw Hill Education

THIS BOOK IS THE PROPERTY OF:

STATE ____________________
PROVINCE ____________________
COUNTY ____________________
PARISH ____________________
SCHOOL DISTRICT ____________________
OTHER ____________________

Book No. __________
Enter information in spaces to the left as instructed

ISSUED TO	Year Used	CONDITION	
		ISSUED	RETURNED

PUPILS to whom this textbook is issued must not write on any page or mark any part of it in any way, consumable textbooks excepted.

1. Teachers should see that the pupil's name is clearly written in ink in the spaces above in every book issued.
2. The following terms should be used in recording the condition of the book: New; Good; Fair; Poor; Bad.